TEACHING
THE PERSISTENT
NON-SWIMMER

by the same author

ACQUIRING BALL SKILL—A Psychological
Interpretation

TEACHING
THE PERSISTENT
NON-SWIMMER

a scientific approach

☆

H. T. A. WHITING

M.A., PH.D., D.L.C.

Department of Physical Education
University of Leeds, England

ILLUSTRATED BY
G. E. B. WHITING

ST. MARTIN'S PRESS
NEW YORK

Library of Congress Catalog Card No.: 70–106413

AFFILIATED PUBLISHERS: Macmillan & Company, Ltd., London
also at Bombay, Calcutta, Madras and Melbourne
The Macmillan Company of Canada, Limited, Toronto

Printed in Great Britain

Contents

Photographs

Preface

The teaching of non-swimmers to swim has received considerable impetus during the past decade. Much of this has been brought about by an appreciation of the great number of people within our island population who cannot swim and the mounting of large scale programmes (particularly by such bodies as the Central Council of Physical Recreation) designed to tackle the problem. Such attempts to minimise the *number* of non-swimmers is not however the only major step which has been taken. There have been considerable changes in attitude in the qualitative approach to the teaching of swimming, and particularly towards the variety of approaches adopted in such teaching. While some of this revised outlook has arisen from an appreciation of individual differences and hence the inappropriateness of particular methods for particular people, it is the work of enlightened teachers within this country which has made such progress meaningful. Winifred Gibson's shallow-water method has considerable merit and its wider adoption has probably only been prevented by the lack of suitable pools for the purpose. It would be difficult to single out individuals who have brought about changes in attitude towards a more enlightened approach to a variety of possible methods of learning to swim and for a child-centred approach to the problem. Such changes are rather reflected in an overall movement from many quarters. However, mention must be made of the contribution of 'Bert' Kinnear prior to and during his appointment as National Technical Officer to the Amateur Swimming Association. His influence both in this country and abroad is still bearing fruit.

In addition to embracing diverse methods of instruction, there has developed a more tolerant attitude towards the use of artificial aids where a decade ago they might have been frowned upon.

It would appear, on the face of it, that children need no longer be subjected to some of the terrifying experiences that were the misfortune of many of their forebears. But, this is not quite the whole story. While learning to swim is a comparatively easy thing for the majority of children, there are still a reasonably large number of children who have difficulty even with the enlightened methods already mentioned It is necessary therefore to define two main categories amongst groups of children or adults attending for any course of swimming instruction:

CATEGORY 1   Those who *have received extended previous instruction* and are still unable to swim

CATEGORY 2   Those who have *never* received previous instruction

Amongst those in Category 2, a percentage will eventually move into Category 1—the remainder will become swimmers.

It is to people who fall into Category 1 that the term 'persistent non-swimmer' is applied in this book. It is further suggested that such people require particular attention if learning to swim is to become anything but a dispiriting, unhappy and often ineffective process. While once again there may be a number of methods by which such children can be taught, there is some merit in having a method designed to combat the difficulties they encounter. The major difficulty here of course being that of *fear*.

While all teachers of swimming would benefit from a knowledge of the physical and psychological factors affecting the non-swimmer, such knowledge is essential to the teacher of the *persistent* non-swimmer. Furthermore, if more teachers of swimming possessed such knowledge, it is likely that there would be fewer persistent non-swimmers. The teacher must be capable of putting himself or herself in the position of the learner, to appreciate the type of body image that the learner is receiving, to experience in the same way that the learner is experiencing. In the process of growth and development and the easy relationship established with the water medium, it will normally be difficult for the teacher to recall such experiences. He needs to re-educate himself with a knowledge of the factors which are likely to influence the behaviour of learner swimmers.

This book sets out to analyse in terms which most teachers of swimming can understand, the physical and psychological factors which influence the person learning to swim. It continues with a method (elaborated in detail) which has proved highly successful in teaching persistent non-swimmers to swim and which has been designed to take advantage of the knowledge given in the early chapters. It is not the only method which might be advocated, but it is suggested that it is a very efficient method and which once understood is easily applied and produces excellent results. While the method has been used with very young children and older people who are not persistent non-swimmers and again has proved highly successful and easy to apply, it is not suggested that the teacher should *necessarily* restrict himself or herself to one such method with this category of non-swimmer.

In talking about teaching people to swim, it is necessary

to define what is meant by a swimmer. In this context, a swimmer is defined as follows:

'A person who has the ability to cross a selected distance in the water in a *relaxed* and *confident* manner *at will* and without any need to struggle or show signs of distress at any stage.'

Compare this with the criterion adopted by many swimming teachers, namely, when the individual concerned can struggle across a given distance with his feet off the bottom making some semblance of a stroke.

A distinction is being made here, between teaching non-swimmers to swim and teaching swimmers (as defined) specific strokes. The former is comparatively easy, quick and straightforward by the method proposed while the latter takes a long time and requires a great deal of application on the part of the learner.

The book is divided into chapters on the physical and psychological factors which need to be understood in tackling this problem, with further chapters elaborating the method proposed and the means of progressing to stroke production. While it is not necessary to read and understand the first two chapters before proceeding to the method, it is suggested that the teacher will be better equipped for the job in hand if he does so.

H. T. A. WHITING

Leeds, November 1968

CHAPTER 1

Physical Factors and Their Application

A human body in water is subject to the physical forces which affect any other object in a water medium. While there must be other considerations—since the human body is capable of self-produced movement and changes in the position of its centre of gravity—such physical considerations must be understood.

Some objects float in water while others sink. It is also possible to obtain 'neutral buoyancy' whereby a suitably devised object will stay in a submerged position in which it is put. What determines whether a body will sink or float? It is not the weight of the body alone, but its *density* relative to the water. This is termed the *specific gravity* of the body. It is useful therefore to define these basic terms.

DENSITY:

> The density of a substance is the ratio of the mass of the substance to its volume. Thus, the density of pure water is 1 gm./cu. cm. (since one cubic centimetre of pure water weighs one gramme).

SPECIFIC GRAVITY:

The specific gravity of a substance can be defined as:

$$\frac{\text{the weight of the substance in air}}{\text{the weight of an equal volume of pure water}}$$

and as such, the value of the specific gravity of a substance is the same whatever units are selected. From the definition, it is clear that the specific gravity of pure water is 1 (since 1 c.c. of water weighs 1 gm.), i.e. the specific gravity of pure water is numerically equal to its density in metric units.

Specific Gravity of the Human Body

One of the factors affecting the ability of the human body to float in water will be its specific gravity.

The ability of a body to float partially or totally immersed in water depends on it having a specific gravity less than or equal to that of the water in which it is placed. In swimming, total immersion is not usually important, but it does have application in 'sub-aqua' work where it is sometimes necessary for a diver to achieve 'neutral buoyancy'. The main consideration in the teaching of non-swimmers is whether the body floats or whether it sinks and the conditions which determine such happenings. It should be noted here, that a moving body with a specific gravity greater than that of the water in which it is placed can still maintain a swimming position by virtue of its speed of movement through the water.

In any experimental determination of the specific gravity of the human body, it is necessary to define the 'body' for any specific gravity value assigned. Failure to do so has made several studies of this aspect virtually useless. There are two major considerations in this respect:

1. The 'body' being referred to as excluding all lung capacity, i.e. even in the 'exhaled' position allowance being made for residual air in the lungs. In such cases, specific gravity measures refer to body tissues alone.

2. The 'body' being referred to as including some lung volume. For any worth-while consideration of the

results obtained by this method, it is necessary to specify the amount of lung inflation. As far as the swimmer is concerned there is always *some* air in the lungs. The swimmer can decrease his overall specific gravity by taking in more air and increase it by exhaling.

Experimental Determination of the
Specific Gravity of the Human Body

It is worth while considering some of the work which has been carried out in an attempt to measure the specific gravity of the human body.

The majority of investigators interested in the accurate assessment of the specific gravity of the human body have used the water displacement method, i.e. weighing of the body in air following by weighing in water to determine the upthrust due to the water (with floaters, a weight is carried and this is subtracted from the overall results). With suitable controls, this has proved to give reasonably reliable results.

Spivak[1] was one of the earliest investigators to publish his results. The specific gravity range he obtained was 0·976–1·049. These results cannot be taken as a practical guide because of the number of subjects (14) and the lack of standardisation of the amount of air in the lungs. They are, however, an indication of the type of results to expect and it is worth while at this stage drawing attention to the small variation either side of unity.

Similar findings were reported by Sandon[2] who obtained a range of 0·923–1·002. Work carried out on the specific gravity of women subjects led Sandon to make the observation that floating cannot be achieved in fresh water if the specific gravity of the body is more than 0·9875 and that *all* women have a density of less than this

[1] Spivak, C. D. The specific gravity of the human body. *Archives of Internal Medicine*, 15, 1915.
[2] Sandon, F. A preliminary enquiry into the density of the living human body. *Biometrika*, 16, 1924.

and hence all women can float! In this connection, Sandon was thinking in terms of floating in any position and not necessarily of horizontal floating.

A more sophisticated study on the specific gravity of women was carried out by Davies.[1] She obtained a specific gravity range for a selected group of young women students of 1–1·19. These figures referred to the specific gravity of the female body tissues excluding all lung volume. By inference then, most of this sample of women would sink if there were no air at all in the lungs (i.e. excluding even residual air).

Highmore et al.[2] investigated the specific gravity of 100 male physical education students (who in terms of body-type—primarily mesomorphic—were a select group). This research was concerned with flotation and although specific gravity measurement were recorded, they were not the major consideration. With the lungs fully in-flated, the results obtained indicated that 84% of the sample had a specific gravity less than unity. The remaining 16% of the sample—what are termed con-stitutional non-floaters—would sink to the bottom of the pool even with their lungs full of air. This percentage represents a very high incidence of constitutional non-floaters, and is obviously influenced by the biased sample of physical education students. So much for telling this type of learner swimmer that the water will support him if he lets it!

Perhaps the most sophisticated study carried out to date was that of Behnke[3] on ninety-nine healthy men in military service (age range 20–40 years). All lung

[1] Davies, M. B. The specific gravity of the human body. Unpublished Master's thesis: Wellesley College: 1930.
[2] Highmore, G. et al. Initial investigation into the nature of flotation. Physical Education Journal, 148, 1955.
Highmore, G. et al. The problem of the male non-floater. Physical Education Journal, 148, 1957.
[3] Behnke, A. R. et al. The specific gravity of healthy men. J. Am. Med. Assoc., 118, 1942.

volume was excluded and elaborate controls were observed throughout.   They report a range of 1·021–1·097 for this group.   The implication here is that in fresh water, the adult male would not be capable of floating in any position without residual air in the lungs and a proportion would be incapable of doing so even with residual air present (as Highmore *et al.* indeed found).

In a study of flotation, Rozelle & Hellebrandt[1] measured a group of twenty-seven young adult women all of whom were expert swimmers.   Their results led them to conclude that:

1.   Not all women can float in fresh water.

2.   If the volume of air in the lungs is increased, the specific gravity of the body is lowered and its floating ability improved.

3.   The angle of flotation depends upon the distance between the centres of buoyancy and weight (see page 10).

Apparently the only study which has looked at changes in specific gravity with age is that of Zook.[2]   This aspect can be of some considerable importance in the teaching of swimming to persons of differing ages.   Zook used a sample of 164 males between the ages of 5 and 19 years. His results are illustrated in Fig. 1.   Specific gravity measurements were carried out both in the fully inspired position and after a maximum expiration.   But, some children at the lower ages were unable to exhale as fully as the older children so that little account can be taken of the specific gravity of the younger children (5–8 years) in the expired lung position.   Attention is drawn to the

[1] Rozelle, R. & Hellebrandt, F.   The floating ability of women.   *Res. Quart.* 8, 1937.
[2] Zook, D. E.   The physical growth of boys.   *Am. J. Dis. Child.*, 43, 1932.

apparent marked decrease in specific gravity between 9 + and 11 + years.

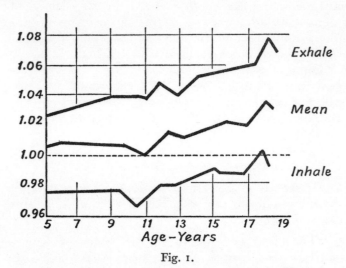

Fig. 1.

It is possible to summarise the suggestions that come from studies such as those quoted in the following way:

1.   The majority of males and females will float in water with a full inhalation.

2.   The majority of males will sink without air in excess of residual air in the lungs.   Women will show less tendency to do so.

3.   Some males will float while breathing 'normally' while others will sink in this condition.

4.   There are particular age ranges for male and female at which floating ability will be the easiest and others where floating with a particular degree of lung inflation will be impossible.

5.   Some adult females will float even without residual air in the lungs.

6. There will be a difference in floating ability between men and women.

In an attempt to clarify some of these issues, it is useful to look at two studies by Whiting[1] designed to examine variations in floating ability with age in the male and female. But before doing this it is necessary for the reader to be aware of differences in floating position and the mechanical factors which influence equilibrium.

The Mechanics of Floating
Equilibrium of the Floating Body

Consider a body in the 'tuck' position (Fig. 2) in water. By definition, if the specific gravity of the body (with a given amount of lung inflation) is greater than that of the water, the body will sink. If, however, the specific gravity is less than that of the water, the body will float in the water with a certain volume of the body above the water. The resultant horizontal forces on the submerged part of the body are zero since the horizontal thrusts of the water balance amongst themselves (being equal in all directions). The only other forces acting on the body are its weight acting downwards through the centre of gravity[2] (G) of the body and the upthrust of the water in which it is floating (P). The latter is in accordance with the familiar Principle of Archimedes.[3] The force (P) is equal to the weight of the water which would occupy the volume displaced by the part of the body under the water and it acts through the centre of

[1] Whiting, H. T. A.   Variations in floating ability with age in the male. *Res. Quart.* 34, 1963.
    Whiting, H. T. A.   Variations in floating ability with age in the female. *Res. Quart.* 36, 1965.
    [2] Centre of Gravity—the point through which the weight of the body can be considered to act.
    [3] When a body is totally or partially immersed in a fluid, it experiences an upthrust equal to the weight of the fluid displaced.

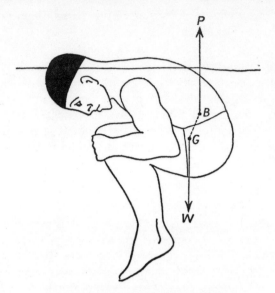

Fig. 2. 'Tuck' float before rotation.

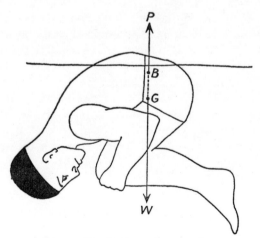

Fig. 3. 'Tuck' float after rotation.

gravity of the displaced water.   The point through which
force (*P*) acts is known as the centre of buoyancy.

Reference to Fig. 2 will indicate that the body is in a
position known as 'unstable equilibrium' since it is under
the stress of two forces acting in opposite directions and
not through the same straight line (a 'couple')—forces
(*P*) and (*W*).   The body will not remain in this position
if the 'tuck' float is maintained, but will rotate until these
forces are equal and opposite (i.e. until they act in the
same straight line) as in Fig. 3.

The point about which the body rotates is termed the
metacentre (*M*) and its position can be determined by
considering two positions of the body during the course of
rotation as indicated in Fig. 4.   It is worth noting that in

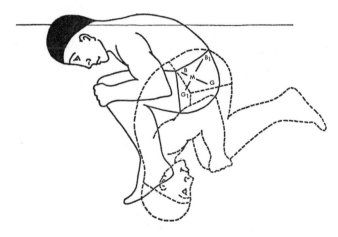

Fig. 4. Position of the metacentre—'M'.

the human body, the position of the centre of buoyancy
and the centre of gravity relative to one another, are
such that the body will always rotate forward and not
backwards in coming to adopt a position of flotation.

Horizontal Flotation

In order for a body to float horizontally, it is necessary for the centre of buoyancy and the centre of gravity to be in the same point or vertically below one another, and for the specific gravity of the body (with a specified lung inflation) to be less than that of the water in which it is floating.

Assuming the body to have a specific gravity less than the water and the position of the centre of gravity and the centre of buoyancy to be out of line with one another, a position of unstable equilibrium will exist as shown in Fig. 5. If left in this position, the body will rotate in the

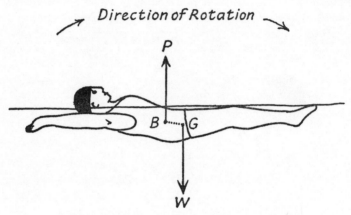

Fig. 5. Horizontal floating position (artificial).

direction shown until the centre of gravity and the centre of buoyancy of the body are vertically in line with one another. The body will continue to float in this new position providing that the breathing organs are clear of the water to enable breathing (Fig. 6). Observation of some people trying to float horizontally will confirm that the legs sink until the body is virtually in a vertical position. With others, the legs remain at the surface without effort. All kinds of intermediate positions will occur.

Consideration of these mechanical principles leads to

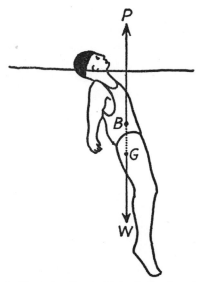

Fig. 6. Rotation from the horizontal position.

the following suggestions for improving the capacity of
the body for horizontal floating when it is incapable of
doing so under normal circumstances:

1.   Raise the centre of gravity of the body by placing
the arms above the head and in the water.   The further
they are raised until they are in line with the body, the
more the centre of gravity is raised.

2.   Flexion of the wrists in (1) so that the hands[1] are
clear of the water and hence no longer supported
by it.   This will increase the weight towards the top
part of the body thus raising the centre of gravity and
reducing the turning force of the couple.

3.   Shallow breathing will prevent over-inflation of the
lungs (which has the effect of raising the specific gravity

[1] Further help in terms of increasing the turning force could be achieved
by taking more of the arm out of water, but this is likely to affect the overall
stability of the body.

towards the top part of the body, increasing the tendency of the body to rotate). The difficulty with this procedure is that, if the air in the lungs becomes very much decreased, the specific gravity of the body may be greater than that of the water in which it is attempting to float, resulting in it sinking.

There are other methods—such as depressing the diaphragm—but they usually involve undue effort on the part of the would-be floater.

With these considerations in mind, it is possible to return to Whiting's (1963, 1965) findings on the relative floating ability of male and female in the horizontal and tuck positions at varying ages.

Variations in Floating Ability with Age in the Male and Female

The test groups for these investigations comprised 1,040 males between the ages of 9 and 24 years and 876 females between the ages of 10 and 18 years, the majority of whom were in full-time attendance at school or university. Although all the test group were swimmers and in the main not nervous of the water, the very nature of some of the tests (total submersion for up to 15 secs) limited the number of performers in the 9- to 10-year group of boys.

All the tests were carried out in an indoor heated swimming pool. The specific gravity of the chlorinated water at the temperature used (79°–84°) differed insignificantly from unity. Performers in the nude (boys) or in costumes and caps (girls) were required to carry out the four tests of flotation given below. In Tests 1, 2 and 3, the subjects were asked to maintain the tuck position to a count of ten to give sufficient time for the final position of the body to be observed. A positive float was recorded if, at the end of this time, the subject was not at the bottom of the pool or in the process of descending.

position of the metacentre—variations in the range of movement at shoulder girdle amongst the subjects prevented the adoption of a standardised position.) Subjects were required to stand in the water at waist height, to sink their shoulders under water, and gently to adopt a horizontal floating position on the back as described. As the test was carried out individually and the performers experienced no breathing discomfiture, oral corrections could be made when the position was inaccurate.

Results for the Male Population

Performers aged 18 and upwards, showed insignificant variations in their floating ability and were consequently bracketed together as one group which might suitably be considered as physically adult.

The results at all age levels for Test 1 ('tuck' float with lungs fully inflated) indicated an almost 100% ability to float in this position.   From 14 to 24 years an occasional true 'sinker' (a person unable to float even with the lungs fully inflated) was found, but the numbers in any one year age range were too few to make worth-while comparisons (seven were recorded in the test group of 1,040).   Their presence should not be overlooked, as individuals of this kind will turn up in learner-swimmer situations.   It is no use telling them that if they lie on the water it will support them!

Fig. 7 gives the percentage of 'tuck' floaters during normal respiration.   There was a significant difference between the numbers of floaters in the 9–13 year age range when compared with all other age groups tested. The decrease in 'tuck' floating ability from 13 years onward indicates a specific gravity of the body (including some lung volume) greater than unity in an increasing percentage of the population.

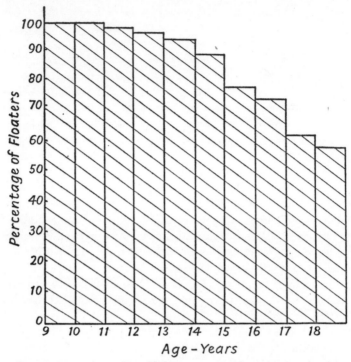

Fig. 7. Percentage of 'tuck' floaters, normal respiration (male)

The percentage of 'tuck' floaters after a maximum exhalation is given diagrammatically in Fig. 8. A highly significant increase in the percentage of floaters occurs between the ages of 10 and 13 years (it will also be recalled that this was implicit in the work of Zook (page 6).

Marked variations from age to age in horizontal floating ability are apparent from Fig. 9. The most significant characteristics of these results are the relatively high percentage of horizontal floaters between the ages of 10 and 13 years and the very small percentage from 13 years onwards. The test group produced no horizontal floaters from 16 years onwards.

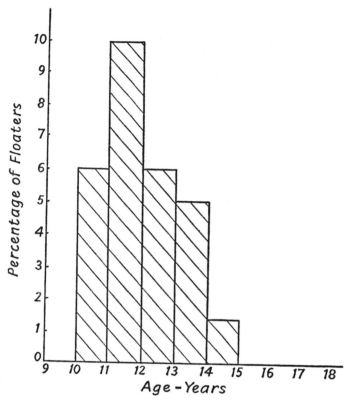

Fig. 8. Percentage of 'tuck' floaters after a maximum exhalation (male)

Results for the Female Population

The results for Test 1 ('tuck' float with lungs fully inflated) indicated almost a 100% ability to float in this position at all the age levels tested. Only one true 'sinker' was recorded—a female of 14 years.

The number of 'tuck' floaters during normal respiration is given in Table 2 (p. 19). These results again indicate almost a 100% ability to 'tuck' float during normal

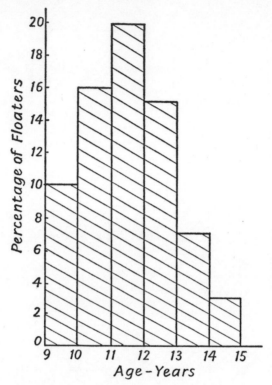

Fig. 9. Percentage of 'horizontal' floaters (male)

respiration. It should however be noted that sinkers in this position do occur. It would be unwise with such a small percentage of 'sinkers' to draw inferences regarding changes in specific gravity of the female body from age range to age range. Useful information can be obtained by a comparison of the 'tuck' floating ability of the male during normal respiration and the results obtained for the female. There is a highly significant difference between the floating ability of the male and female during normal respiration over the age range 10–18 years.

TABLE 2

Number of Floaters and Non-Floaters for Each Year of Age Range Tested

Age (Years)	Horizontal Float		'Tuck' Float Full inspiration		'Tuck' Float Normal breathing		'Tuck' Float Maximum Exhalation	
	Float	Non-Float	Float	Non-Float	Float	Non-Float	Float	Non-Float
10–11	9	37	46	–	45	–	1	18
11–12	21	118	141	–	140	–	14	107
12–13	25	81	106	–	105	–	8	80
13–14	20	177	197	–	181	3	16	127
14–15	17	150	176	1	171	6	17	129
15–16	18	85	103	–	97	2	6	58
16–17	10	48	58	–	58	–	4	32
17–18	4	45	49	–	47	–	1	33
	124	741	876	1	844	12	67	584
Excluded 'No-test'	11		–		21		226	

Table 2 also gives the number of 'tuck' floaters after a maximum exhalation. Unfortunately, no implications can be drawn from the results of this test as 25% of the sample recorded a no-test. In spite of the sample being sophisticated swimmers, this test presented difficulties which were not apparent when testing a similar male population. This may be a characteristic fault of the relatively unsophisticated female swimmer, or it may merely reflect a characteristic fault in the sample used.

Variations from age to age in horizontal floating ability are apparent from Fig. 10. There are highly significant variations in the distribution suggesting that in the female there is a decrease in horizontal floating ability between the ages of 13 and 15 and at 17 + years with corresponding increases between 10 and 13 years and 15 and 17 years.

A comparison of these results with those obtained for the male in the horizontal floating position indicated

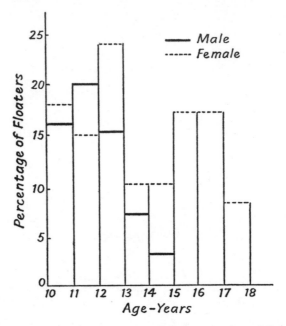

Fig. 10. Percentages of 'horizontal' floaters (male and female)

significant differences in horizontal floating ability between the male and female during the age range 10–18 years. Moreover, a comparison of the floating ability of male and female between the ages of 10 and 13 years indicates no significant differences. Thus, it would appear, that the differences in horizontal floating ability between male and female reported above are mainly reflected in the differences which occur from the age of 13 onwards.

The following conclusions can be drawn from the studies on the male and female reported above which are likely to be of help in developing any technique of swimming instruction:

1. Putting the non-swimmer in the picture

2 and 3. The float in position

4. Getting used to the float—shoulders under the water, 'bobbing' off the bottom of the pool

5. *Stage 1.* Basic starting position—bend the knees until the shoulders are under the water

6. *Stage 2.* Head back on the float and resting on the water, eyes looking directly overhead

7. *Stage 3.* Hips beginning to extend, arms relaxed by side

8. *Stage 4.* Hips extending, feet leaving the bottom of the pool

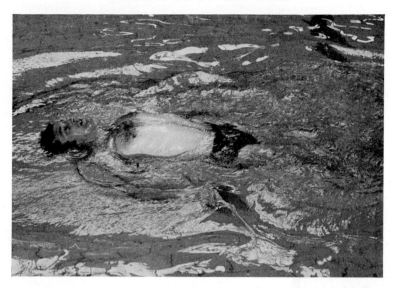

9. *Stage 5.* Horizontal position almost achieved. N.B. how head and chest are clear of the water and hips in full extension

10. *Stage 6.* The correct position for beginning the leg-kick

11. Starting the leg-kick. Legs almost straight, ankle extended; kick fast and shallow

12. *Stage 1.* Stop kicking and allow the legs to sink while keeping the head in correct position

13. *Stage 2.* Legs beginning to sink

14. *Stage 3.* Legs near the bottom of the pool in a position to initiate a forward-bending movement to attain a standing position

15. *Stage 4.* The movement completed prior to standing up

1. A marked decrease in the percentage of male floaters from the age of 13 years onwards.

2. A pronounced peak in both horizontal and 'tuck' floating ability of the male between the ages of 10 and 13 years.

3. An almost complete incapacity of the male for horizontal floating from about 15 years and onwards.

4. The presence of a few male 'sinkers' between the ages of 14 and 18 + years and of one female 'sinker' at the 14 + age level.

5. Superior 'tuck' floating ability of the female between the ages of 10 and 18 years as compared with the male over a similar age range.

6. Peaks in horizontal floating ability of the female between the ages of 10 and 13 years and 15 and 17 years with corresponding increases in horizontal floating ability between the ages of 13 and 15 years and from 17 + years.

7. Superior horizontal floating ability of the female from the age of about 13 years onwards as compared with the male of a similar age.

The decreased floating ability in the 'tuck' position and the almost complete incapacity to float horizontally in the male from the age of 15 years onwards, are important factors to be considered in the teaching of swimming and life saving to adults and older male children. These factors do indeed suggest the advantage, and in some instances the necessity, of using artificial aids to buoyancy when teaching males of 13 + years to swim.

c

CHAPTER 2

Psychological Factors affecting the
Non-Swimmer

In the preface to this book, it was suggested that one of the reasons why a more enlightened approach to the teaching of non-swimmers had come about was a greater appreciation of the psychological implications of individual differences. While this is certainly the case, it is still clear that such an appreciation has not been extended far enough. Non-swimmers of all categories are grouped together for initial instruction in the learner swimmer situation. While this is partly due to the limitations of time and facilities, it must be appreciated that part of the difficulty is a lack of awareness on the part of the swimming teacher of the harm that can be done to many children in such a setting and the reinforcement of any previous misgivings they might have had. Minority groups suffer in this instance as in many others.

It does seem reasonably clear that the persistent non-swimmer is not so because he lacks the potential for developing the physical skill of swimming. It would be almost true to say that the skill aspect of swimming can be acquired by all but the very severely disabled and, even here, the extent of such disablement would need to be fairly diffuse. The root cause of the inability is almost entirely fear of the water or of the swimming situation itself. This of course is not a new observation, but is probably the most potent factor in making the learning of swimming very difficult for some people. The problem, then, in teaching the persistent non-swimmer, is removing or alleviating the fear involved and not the difficulty of acquiring the skill technique. In teaching any children or adults who come into Category 2 outlined in the preface, one of the aims of the teacher should be the prevention of fear being acquired by the way in which the situation is structured and handled. It is not possible to lay down hard and fast rules as to how this can be done, but it is possible to discuss the development of fear responses and methods by which they might be tackled. In so doing, it is hoped that the teacher may gain a more sophisticated insight into what needs to be done and arrange his procedures accordingly.

Fear and Anxiety

It is useful to differentiate first of all between *fear* and *anxiety*. The usual distinction made is that fear is more closely related to an object, idea or situation, whereas anxiety is of a more diffuse nature.[1]

One of the difficulties with fear, is that people do not always make their fear manifest. Such patterns of behaviour can persist throughout life—the person showing outward calm but being inwardly in a high state of tension. Some of the children normally accepted as confident and 'at home' in the water, may be far more tense and afraid than some of the apparently timid children and need as much understanding.

There are usually two main methods of dealing with a frightening situation—running away from it once there, or not going! Mowrer[2] terms these *active* and *passive* avoidance behaviour. With a captive population such as exists in schools learning to swim is often compulsory. Many children, if they are afraid of water will do their

[1] Zangwill, O. L. *An Introduction to Psychology.* London: Methuen, 1950.
[2] Mowrer, O. H. *Learning theory and the symbolic process.* New York: Wiley, 1960.

best to bring about passive avoidance by devious means. These are the signs that the understanding teacher should recognise and treat with sympathy. There will still be children who suppress their fears and suffer accordingly.

In the psychological literature, fear is considered to be a 'drive' because it motivates behaviour (although in the case of passive avoidance, the person is motivated not to do something!). Sometimes, it can be a positive drive to learning if not too severe and, at others, a negative drive. What is certain, is that the anxiety level differs with individuals and will thus have varying effects on performance.

Individual Differences

Consideration of individual differences in the literature usually goes under the heading of personality assessment or personality theory. This particular area of psychology has a long history and there have been numerous books produced on the topic. Some approaches have been speculative while others are based on reasonably well established experimental evidence. Personality theory is concerned with the description of individual differences according to some structured framework. Although differing in their theoretical approaches, there is strong agreement amongst workers in this field that personality is the resultant of environmental forces acting on hereditary potential and hence consideration of *learning* plays an important part in any consideration of personality development.

In the present context, it is suggested that fear of water or the swimming situation is a *learned phenomenon* although the person may possess hereditary predispositions which affect the way in which fear is acquired. The assumption that fear of water is not innate is based on the absence of such reports to this effect, and also the common observation that the very young baby in the arms of a *confident* mother or nurse shows pleasure rather than fear when in contact with water. Whether or not fear is acquired will depend on the handling of the child in the water situation. Thus, fear of water may be the result of a number of years of relatively unpleasant water experience or the result of a single traumatic experience (as will be elaborated later in the chapter).

Conditioning

While the majority of learning theorists accept the phenomenon of 'conditioning' as a form of learning, they differ in the relative importance they attach to the classical conditioning process as elaborated by Pavlov.[1] Some theorists—notably Mowrer—reduce all learning to a conditioning procedure while others attach relatively little importance to it. Since this chapter is mainly concerned with fear conditioning in relation to personality development and hence to its implication for the teaching of non-swimmers, some time will be spent on elaborating the process of conditioning.

In order to understand the way in which conditioned responses are formed, it is instructive to look at what has now become a classical experiment carried out by Watson[2] in 1920.

As is well known, a sudden loud noise will evoke a spontaneous fear reaction in a young child—the degree of reaction varying with the individual. The loud noise is said to be an unconditional stimulus as it produces the fear response automatically. Watson chose for his experiment, a young boy who had never shown any spontaneous fear of a rabbit or other furry animal. The rabbit was brought near to the child who manifested a positive reaction by reaching out for

[1] Pavlov, I. P. *Conditioned reflexes.* London: O.U.P., 1927.
[2] Watson, J. B. & Rayner, R. Conditioned emotional reactions. *J. Exp. Psych.*, 3, 1920.

it. At the moment when the child's hand was stretched out to take the rabbit, a sudden loud noise was made behind the child—the source of the noise being unknown to the child. He reacted by showing fear. After a number of pairings of the rabbit (conditional stimulus—CS) and the loud noise (unconditional stimulus—US) the *sight* of the rabbit called forth the same signs of fear and avoidance. The child had developed a conditioned fear to the rabbit where previously such a fear had not existed.

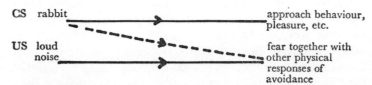

In addition to the formation of a conditioned response to a particular stimulus (such as the rabbit in Watson's experiment), it is also found in conditioning procedures that once such a response is established, stimuli which are similar to the CS will establish the same response but to a lesser degree. This is termed stimulus generalisation. For example, in addition to the fear of the rabbit in the example quoted, the fear also generalised to other similar objects (e.g. a piece of fur material), the amount of generalisation depending upon the degree of similarity amongst the objects. This example demonstrates simply how fear may be acquired in the laboratory situation and it is easy to understand how similar fears may be acquired in everyday life either on the basis of purely fortuitous circumstances or in some predetermined fashion. Moreover, while some of the conditioned responses may have a survival value (such as conditioned fear of poisonous snakes), others lead to completely irrational fears. In the case of 'Little Albert' there was no real need to be afraid of a tame rabbit.

Generally speaking, in the conditioning procedure described, the number of times that the CS is paired with the US determines the degree of conditioning. Another factor also has to be taken into account. This has been termed autonomic lability—reflecting the way in which the autonomic nervous system responds to a particular stimulus. It is fairly easy to understand how in the above model the same amount of noise might induce different autonomic responses in different people. Thus, from the point of view of the acquisition of a conditioned response, it is useful to consider two main contributory factors:

1. The ease with which conditioning takes place
2. The autonomic lability of the person's nervous system

While a number of personality theorists have incorporated ideas of conditioning into their theories, it is Eysenck[1] in particular who has done pioneering work in this area of personality research. He has related the ease with which conditioning takes place to the personality dimension of introversion/extraversion and the autonomic lability of a person to the dimension of neuroticism. Eysenck has shown that a predisposition towards both neuroticism (stable/unstable) and introversion/extraversion is inherited. The behaviour of a person is determined by the way in which environmental circumstances interact with such predispositions.

It follows from Eysenck's theory, that people towards the extraverted end of an introversion/extraversion dimension will form conditioned responses slowly and with difficulty and once they are formed they will be relatively easy to get rid of while people towards the

[1] Eysenck, H. J. *The biological basis of personality*, London, Routledge & Kegan Paul, 1968.

introverted end of the dimension should form conditioned responses quickly and once formed such responses should be relatively enduring. In addition, a person's standing on the neuroticism dimension will be determined by the autonomic lability of his nervous system.

It is now possible to summarise much of what has been outlined in this chapter in the following way:

Suggestions have been made as to how fear reactions can be developed and how they may be adaptive or maladaptive depending to a large extent on the circumstances prevailing at the time. Eysenck has also suggested that the extravert will condition with difficulty and the introvert more easily. Thus, already there is the suggestion that in similar fear conditioning situations the introvert will be more likely to be affected (in terms of developing conditioned fear responses) than the more extraverted person. These are considerations which might prove useful in connection with the learning of skills in fear situations. Similarly, because of differences in autonomic lability, a particular fear invoking stimulus will have different effects on different individuals.

In the light of this information, it is now possible to return to an example taken from everyday life which demonstrates the way in which fear of water might become conditioned. Bentler[1] recently reported a case of fear conditioning within a water situation. It should be noted that, while it was stated earlier that the number of reinforced trials determines to a large extent the strength of the conditioned response, this does not preclude *single trial* conditioning where the fear produced on one single occasion is very pronounced. In such circumstances, a *traumatic event* is being referred to. Bentler reports how a

[1] Bentler, P. M. An infant's phobia treated with reapproval inhibition therapy. *J. Child. Psych. & Psychiat.*, 3, 1962.

year-old female child acquired phobic reactions to water after slipping in a bathtub. Up to that time, water and bathing had been enjoyable experiences. After the traumatic event, the child would not go near water in any circumstances. Some form of therapy in such an extreme case was necessary. The phobia developed by the child after this single experience was of course a maladaptive response as there is no *real* need to be afraid of water, even of being submerged. Bentler obviously accepted this idea, because he carried out a clinical procedure to remove the unnecessary fear by a process of inhibition therapy which might be considered to be an application of sports medicine even at such a limited age!

One fact which stands out from Bentler's article is how fear of water can be developed at such an early age and if not counter-conditioned either deliberately or through everyday occurrences in life such a fear may persist right up to adulthood and its effect on the ability to learn to swim be most pronounced. The case quoted is of course an extreme one and there are all forms of variation right down to the person who has no fear of the water under any circumstances.

It might be asked at this stage how conditioned fears can be got rid of once acquired. But perhaps the primary consideration is to prevent them being acquired in the first place! This is easier said than done, as it seems likely that such fears begin to be developed at a very early age. What would seem to be required is education of parents so that they are aware of the difficulties involved and how their own personality (including fear of water) may affect the learning of their children.

The normal procedure for getting rid of conditioned responses in the laboratory is either the process of *extinction* or that of *counter-conditioning*. In the former case the conditioned stimulus (CS) is presented without the unconditioned stimulus (US) until the response disappears. There will be periods when the response spontaneously recovers but it will usually be at a lower level. In everyday language, it would be said that the presentation of the stimulus situation without the reinforcement for a sufficient number of occasions will result in the conditioned response being lessened or removed altogether. People do not generally go on making unnecessary responses in the absence of reinforcement. In the case of counter-conditioning, an attempt is made (or occurs naturally) to condition another response which is incompatible with the first one. Take for example once again, Bentler's infant. Bentler reasoned that the child had developed a conditioned fear of water mediated as would be expected by the sympathetic branch of the autonomic nervous system. If therefore he could condition a parasympathetic response which was incompatible with fear, it was likely that in the situation the fear would disappear, since both responses (fear and hope) could not exist at the same time towards the same situation. This is precisely what he set out to and succeeded in doing. The counter conditioning procedure adopted by Bentler involved attraction towards toys and bodily contact with the mother while the child was near water to elicit responses which were presumed to be incompatible with anxiety.

From what has been said about the acquisition of conditioned responses, it will be clear that fear of the water may be the result of a number of years of relatively unpleasant water experience or the result of a single traumatic experience as exemplified in Bentler's study. In terms of the personality theory discussed, it follows that although extraverted people may be difficult to condition, a series of unpleasant water experiences (i.e. continual fear reinforcement) may indeed produce a conditioned fear reaction although it is unlikely to be as severe as a similar set of experiences in the more introverted person. Hence, in as far as our culture presents similar water situations to individuals, it is more *probable* that the more introverted person will develop conditioned fear of water.

To determine whether or not there was such a relationship between personality dimensions in Eysenck's terms and persistent non-swimmers, Whiting & Stembridge[1] carried out an investigation on large numbers of schoolboys between the ages of 11 and 12 years. The results showed a highly significant relationship between introversion and children classified as persistent non-swimmers. Some significant differences were also found with respect to neuroticism in persistent non-swimmers. The results are summarised in Table 3. The relationship found

TABLE 3

Extraversion Score Means and Standard Deviations on the Junior Maudsley Personality Inventory in a sample of Secondary Schoolboys

Age	Subjects	Number	Neuroticism			Extraversion/Introversion		
			Mean Score	S.D.		Mean Score	S.D.	
11	Non-swimmers	104	8·16	3·79	Highly Signif. Diff.	10·41	3·25	Highly Signif. Diff.
	Swimmers	653	6·80	3·33		11·77	3·12	
12	Non-swimmers	86	7·63	3·54	Signif. Diff.	10·70	3·51	Highly Signif. Diff.
	Swimmers	804	6·70	3·31		11·91	3·18	

between neuroticism and introversion and persistent non-swimmers is in line with Eysenck's contention of the dual nature of anxiety, i.e. that anxiety in the learning situation may be contributed to by high neuroticism as well as by ease of conditioning.

[1] Whiting, H. T. A. & Stembridge, D. E.   Personality and the persistent non-swimmer.   *Res. Quart.* 36, 3, 1965.

What do these considerations suggest from the point of view of the teaching of persistent non-swimmers? Bentler's patient was lucky; the trauma was so pronounced that therapy was necessary at the time and the child was apparently cured of her fears and was able to take kindly to water soon after therapy was completed. Many cases —usually of a less severe nature—do not have specific therapy and often circumstances in life do not permit the fear to be resolved. These are probably the children or adults who can be found who could not be coaxed anywhere near a swimming pool, and often as a consequence develop other emotional symptoms with the result that they are excused swimming instruction if they are at school. It would not be surprising if they later communicated such fears to *their* children. Others with lesser fears use every means at their disposal to avoid being exposed to the fear situation and having such fear reinforced.

Thus, the first thing that suggests itself is that when teaching skills in a fear situation, teachers must indeed be careful with their 'programming'. There will obviously be children or adults amongst non-swimmer groups who condition easily, and with the wrong 'programme' it is possible to produce an enhanced fear response and, as a consequence, a general antipathy towards the activity in question.

With persistent non-swimmers, it is assumed that fear of water has been retained because of previous unpleasant experiences which have resulted in conditioned fear being acquired (it is worth noting also that verbal conditioning by over-protective parents can achieve similar results), and that life has not provided the necessary situations for extinction or counter-conditioning of their fear. With such people, it would seem desirable that any method used should aim at counter-conditioning the acquired fear. This may need to be a deliberate therapeutic procedure with extreme cases or may take the form of the right 'programming' in the teaching situation.

For persistent non-swimmers, in particular, the aim should be to provide teaching methods which condition 'hope' and not 'fear'. In general, this implies that putting the non-swimmer in a position in which he is likely to fail should be avoided. This, of course, raises all the topics of artificial aids, warm and shallow water, etc. However, being *aware* of the problem and the issues involved, it is more likely that the 'programming' of a course of instruction will be more capable of producing desirable results than if the problem is approached without prior knowledge. These issues are tackled in the next chapter in which a method of procedure is described.

CHAPTER 3

Teaching the Persistent Non-Swimmer

The previous chapters have outlined the physical and psychological factors which are considered to be of importance in the teaching of non-swimmers. The problem which now poses itself, is that of finding an efficient method of approach to people who show persistent difficulty in learning to swim and one which takes account of the previous findings.

One of the arguments often put up against the introduction of a 'new' method, is that it is the *teacher* who is of supreme importance and the *method* very much a secondary consideration. It must be admitted here, that the very good teacher is likely to succeed even with limited methods available. This does not deny that such teachers are likely to be even more efficient and better equipped if, in addition to their own ability and understanding, they have a method which has proven to be efficient and successful. The less well-equipped teacher, or the teacher at the beginning of his swimming teaching career, will probably find the information which has been given so far to be invaluable and the presentation of a suitable method of approach, a good starting point. The method to be elaborated in this chapter has received considerable testing over a number of years and has proved its worth from the point of view of success with both adult and child persistent non-swimmers and also with very young children who have as yet not encountered difficulties in the water situation. Although the procedure in this method has been worked out and refined during this time, it is not suggested that even at this stage it has reached its ultimate in sophistication. It is suggested that teachers might like to try it in the way that it is laid down and adjust particular procedures in accordance with their own findings and their own personality.

It has already been emphasised that the learning of some physical activities—in particular gymnastics and swimming—not only requires that the performer acquire the necessary physical skill, but that he does so in a situation where fear is likely to be present. Thus, the acquisition of skill is restricted by this overriding fear. The acquisition of skill cannot be divorced from the limiting factor of fear and any teaching approach must deal with both problems. The obvious solution to this problem is 'never to put the learner in a situation in which he is likely to fail'. This is not entirely possible, but should be the overriding consideration of any method of approach with persistent non-swimmers in particular and with non-swimmers in general. Learning theorists in psychology have for some time emphasised the need for continual positive reinforcement in the learning situation. This in effect is one of the principles underlying programmed learning. The student is successively placed in situations in which he is most likely to make the correct response. This approach is equally important in the teaching of physical skills and is something that the very good teacher does automatically.

It seems likely—as suggested in the last chapter—that the introverted non-swimmer of Category 1, because of his lack of confidence in himself and in others, is even more likely to be restricted by his fear of the water than is the extraverted non-swimmer and to be even more in need of a method which enables him to succeed at every stage and thus reinforce his learning in a positive way.

Bearing these points in mind, a tentative answer to the problem of a suitable teaching method suggests:

1. Non-swimmers should be taught in a position which initially does not necessitate the head going under water.

2. They should have the benefit of artificial support to enable them to overcome the lack of confidence they exhibit. (The results of Chapter 1 also suggest that in some cases such artificial support may be a necessity.)

3. They should be able to breathe freely, with little possibility of taking in water.

4. They should work initially in small groups where maximum confidence can be instilled and where interaction with other members who are not learners can be kept to a minimum.

Such suggestions would present difficulties for many of the present orthodox approaches. In designing any method of swimming instruction, it is necessary not only to bear the above factors in mind but also to take account of the variation in floating ability at various ages and between male and female.

Swimming Method

The swimmer in this context (and as outlined in the preface) is considered to be:

'a person who has the ability to cross a selected distance (10 yards) in a relaxed and confident manner at will and without the need to struggle or show signs of distress at any stage.'

A distinction is being made here between teaching non-swimmers to swim and teaching swimmers (as defined) to acquire specific orthodox strokes. The former is easy, quick and straightforward by the method proposed, while the latter takes a long time and requires a good deal of application on the part of the stroke learner.

Artificial Aids

It is not intended here to enter the controversy over the use of swimming aids—a controversy which occupies the stage from time to time. It is accepted that if an artificial aid produces the desired result quickly it should be used. Practically, such aids have proved their worth and are an integral part of the system to be described. Reference to the experimental work in chapter 1 indicates that, with adults, a significant percentage of 'sinkers' in the normal breathing position occur, and thus artificial aids are virtually essential in teaching such persons to swim, unless the teacher is prepared to let them spend a lot of their learning periods under water! Some support for the use of artificial aids towards learning has come from the studies of 'Guidance training' in the psychological literature. Such procedures—which range from physically putting the learner through the required movement, to merely 'hinting' at the correct response—have proved to be efficient methods of learning. There is always the possibility—as critiques of artificial supports often suggest—that the person will become dependent on such artificial aids. This has sometimes been shown to be the case in laboratory sudies. It will again depend on how the teacher handles the situation and the length of time that the person learning needs to retain such support.

The artificial aid used in this method (others may be suitable or could be devised) consists of a sausage-shaped inflated rubber bladder   enclosed in a cotton bag to which are attached two long fastening tapes (Fig. 11). The position of the inflatable float can be adjusted, but it has

---

[1] A full-size rugby ball bladder with a neck inflator is a useful compromise.

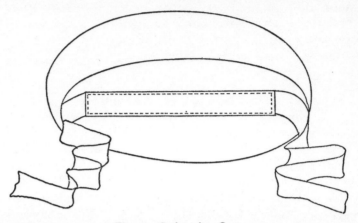

Fig. 11. Swimming float.

been found that tying on the float loosely—with a knot (so that it cannot slip off)—allows the learner while swimming on his back to rest the back of his neck on the float (Fig. 15). This has the advantage of holding the face reasonably clear of the water and the slight disadvantage—particularly in the case of the non-horizontal floater—of causing the legs to lie a little lower in the water and to sink somewhat quicker than might otherwise occur.

The degree of inflation of the float will depend on the individual concerned and the stage of learning reached. Around the 10 to 13 year age group, where floating ability is probably at its best, it may be necessary to only half inflate. The most satisfactory procedure is to inflate the float until three-quarters full and to check the position when the person is in the water. If the float is over-inflated, the subject will lie high in the water and there may be a tendency towards lateral rotation. Over-inflation also increases the tendency towards forward rotation by raising the centre of gravity.

Putting the Non-swimmer in the Picture

Fear will not only be exhibited by the persistent non-swimmer because of his previous experience, it will also be shown by many non-swimmers because of their lack of experience! In this case, it is fear of the unknown reinforced by verbal conditioning of their contemporaries (particularly those who can swim) and 'old wives' tales'.

A short time should always be spent with each group of learners, coming to their first session of tuition in explaining the principles upon which they are being taught and, at the same time, obtaining from them information as to their previous learning experiences and any particular fears and difficulties they have encountered or anticipate. The former can be done as a group, while the latter is better tackled individually, particularly with the introverted person.

All too often, teachers have the tendency to tell their pupils to perform particular actions without giving reasons for their performance. While this may be successful with some persons, it does not always apply. In the main, a procedure of the nature outlined will be found to have worthwhile effects both on the confidence of the performer and in transfer to the swimming situation. In addition, it gives the teacher an opportunity to instil some confidence in himself as a teacher if tackled in the right way. Points particularly worth stressing would seem to be:

1. This method endeavours to overcome the usual fear of 'going under' by making it almost impossible for the head to become submerged unless the non-swimmer wishes it to do so.

2. The elementary theory behind horizontal flotation (depending upon the ages of the group or individuals). By this is meant that they are made aware of the fact that owing to the relative positions of the centre of buoyancy and the centre of gravity of the body

(although not usually in those terms!) it is impossible for the body to rotate backwards under its own forces, so that, if they adopt a back lying position, the legs in over 95% of the cases will sink towards the bottom (the remaining percentage will include the few adult horizontal floaters and the constitutional non-floaters).

3. That they are being taught the back-crawl leg kick in order to overcome the tendency for the legs to sink. The legs therefore in addition to any propulsion they might give, serve to keep the body horizontal.

4. The elementary principles of the back-crawl leg kick are explained in as little detail as possible. They are urged to remember the essentials—kicking from the thigh, relaxed knee, extended ankles, relaxation and shallow kick—and to experiment along these general lines until they find the best method of propulsion (see Chapter 5).

5. The head must be allowed to lie *in* the water in line with the body or slightly extended backwards to help the legs to remain in the horizontal position and to keep the body relaxed[1] and breathing naturally.

These instructions, take less than five minutes. Some of them are probably only suitable for older children and adults. In any case, the method of expanding these principles will depend on the person to whom they are addressed.

Having dealt with the above, and answered any questions which might arise, the beginner is ready to enter the water. Where any choice is available it is suggested that with the adult a depth of three feet is suitable, and with all non-swimmers, it is suggested that the water be really warm—84 F. (usually not the case!).

---

[1] Relaxation is emphasised throughout because of the disrupting effect which unnecessary tension has on the body position, leg kick and breathing. Furthermore, it is difficult for a person to be relaxed and at the same time be over-worried by the situation.

Initial Stages

The float is put on and tied with a knot as previously indicated. Confidence practices in the initial stages have not been found necessary with older children and adults. Younger children will not in general be *persistent* non-swimmers and probably it will be desired to let them use the float and a semblance of the method together with a great deal of free practice. When the learner swimmers have become accustomed to the water and are ready to begin, they are encouraged to test the supporting ability of the float by putting their shoulders underneath the water and bouncing gently off the bottom of the pool without making any attempt to go into a floating position. The learner will feel a tendency for the float to want to take him on to his back but this should not be encouraged at this stage although it is useful to comment on the fact when he rests. (Plates 4–5.)

The Horizontal Position

It must be emphasised that the non-swimmers are not taught to float horizontally—quite the reverse! It has already been shown that few people—particularly adults —can float horizontally with their arms held sideways. With the arm relaxed by the sides (the position to be adopted here) this is even more difficult.

The next stage, is to get the beginner into the back-lying position with as little difficulty as possible and with a minimum chance of the face getting water on to it. This is considered to be one of the most important stages of the method, and the steps in achieving this should be well understood (Plates 6–10):

1. Bend the knees so that the shoulders are under the water and the arms are relaxed and hanging by the sides (the position always adopted at the beginning and the one practised initially in getting used to the float).

2.   Put the head backwards into the water so that the float is acting as a pillow to the neck and the eyes are open and looking directly upwards at the roof/sky. N.B. The feet are still on the bottom of the pool and the knees are bent (Figs. 12 and 13).

3.   The hips are extended *without lifting the head* off the water and the learner adopts a position lying on the water as relaxed as possible, breathing freely.   In water three feet deep, adults usually have no difficulty in doing this.   Children will probably need to give a small push off the bottom of the pool at the same time. The learner should practise this stage until he is able to lie on the water in a relaxed position (judged by the absence of tension in face, arms etc.) with the hips extended (i.e. not sitting in the water) and near the surface of the water before continuing to other stages. This procedure must be mastered if the learning process is to proceed without difficulty.   A number of trials should be carried out until the learner is confident in adopting this position.   It has been found useful to have the swimmer parallel to the side of the pool so that if he is at all worried, he has something on which to hold.   This should not however be encouraged unless the learner cannot proceed in any other way (Figs. 14 & 15).

It should be reiterated here, that part of the purpose of the above is to indicate to the learner that he cannot float horizontally!   This will be clear to the learner when he has adopted the back lying position.   He is encouraged to remain lying relaxed in this position while the legs sink. It is necessary for him to keep the head back all the time with the eyes looking towards the roof/sky until the legs have ceased to rotate.   He may then stand up quite easily under his own volition (or initially by holding the side of the bath) and with little effort on his part.   Practice

Fig. 12. Starting to get into the horizontal position.

Fig. 13. Beginning the hip extension and backward push in order to get into the horizontal floating position.

Fig. 14. Leaving the bottom of the pool—hips maintained in extended position.

Fig. 15. The horizontal position.

should also be given at standing up if it is thought that this will make the learner any happier. (Plates 12–15.)

These stages serve three main functions:

1.   They make the learner aware in a practical way of the underlying principles of the method and the need for a leg kick of the crawl type.

2.   They demonstrate to him a simple method of standing up from the back lying position, i.e. merely to *stop* kicking and allow his legs to sink before making any other movement. It is unlikely that any horizontal floaters will remain because the arms are by the sides and because of the additional lift to the top part of the body given by the float. Where this is found, a more deliberate attempt will be necessary.

3. The learner gains confidence in the ability of the float to support him and is aware of the freedom he has in breathing.

Movement

The learner is now able to adopt the back-lying position in a relaxed manner with hips extended (this in all should take about ten minutes except with extreme cases) and is ready to start on the propulsive stage. All the previous stages are repeated until the time that the learner has adopted a floating position on his back (this procedure is always followed exactly until the learner can confidently get on to his back by any means that he likes). The learner then attempts the back-crawl leg kick which was explained to him before he entered the water (Fig. 16 and Plate 11).

Fig. 16. The back crawl leg kick.

Unless the learner experiences any real difficulty, correction to technique can be avoided as after a short while a propulsive kick is usually obtained. Encouragement at this stage is most beneficial. The greatest reward comes when the learner finds himself moving for the first time.

Once the learner is able to move fairly comfortably, an attempt can be made to make his kick more efficient.

Verbal Correction

One of the primary requirements for the acquisition of skill of any kind is knowledge of results. This may come from information received as a direct result of carrying out the skill itself, or can be artificially supplied by a teacher. It is extremely difficult for any beginner in his new water medium to have a clear idea of the result of his efforts and thus, it is difficult for him to make adjustments which would improve his performance. The beginner must inevitably rely on verbal correction by the teacher. On the front with the head in the water—even without any struggling—the beginner cannot hear the teacher very well, and of course cannot see him. Verbal corrections in this case can only be applied after a beginner has completed a sequence of movements. The beginner on his back can both see and hear (since the head is reasonably high) the teacher and is thus continually able to make adjustments in the light of information received. It will be found, in practice, that gesticulation probably does more to indicate corrections which are necessary than verbal comment.

The type of correction necessary will of course depend on the faults being made.

Faults and their Correction

It should be recalled here that the learner is being taught to swim on his back using the back-crawl leg kick and *without* the use of the arms.

Position of the Head (Plate 18)

The position of the head is one of the main controlling factors. Very often correction of faulty head position is all that is necessary to drastically improve performance. In the learning stages the head should lie comfortably *in* and supported *by* the water. There should be no signs of stress on the face. Where this does occur, the learner's attention can be drawn to this and relaxation emphasised. It is useful to indicate points on the roof of the pool on which the beginner can focus.

Flexion of the head, so that it is looking towards a side wall of the pool, causes the legs to lie low in the water and the kick to be laboured. The latter factor may be the first indication of a faulty head position.

Breathing

Breathing should be natural (i.e. not laboured). This in itself is an aid to relaxation throughout the body. If the lungs are inflated and the breath held, the specific gravity of the upper part of the body is lowered and the legs have a greater tendency to sink. If the beginner breathes out and then holds his breath, his specific gravity may become so high that he becomes submerged or almost submerged. When this latter factor is apparent, it would be wise to consider breathing faults. This is, in fact, particularly true of coloured people whose body specific gravity tends to be high. Breathing, in spite of the breathing organs being clear of the water does play an important part. Corrections to faulty breathing— once this is apparent—are fairly obvious. Usually, it is only necessary to draw the beginner's attention to the fault—if he has not already had this demonstrated to him in a practical way!

It is worth noting that, with advanced learners and others whose body specific gravity is high, the body can be kept fairly high in the water by shallow breathing so that the lungs are kept fairly well inflated all the time.

Body Position

The body position in relation to the legs should be as near horizontal as possible. Slight flexion at hip joint is not detrimental (Fig. 16). The main fault likely to occur here is tension in the abdominal muscles resulting in a Vshaped body position which inevitably leads to the head being lifted and tension throughout the lower body making an efficient kick impossible. The overall impression is of the body sitting in the water (Fig. 17 and Plate 20). This

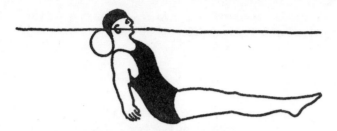

Fig. 17. Failure to extend the hips.

fault often occurs with the person who is tense in the initial starting position and is one of the reasons why the correct starting position with extended hips is emphasised throughout. The fault is easy to recognise by virtue of the semi-sitting position. For correction, it is usually necessary to return to the initial starting position and correct the position from there. With a minor fault, it is often sufficient to draw the attention of the learner to tension in the abdominal muscles and to get him to relax. N.B. This fault rarely occurs with the learner who has mastered the starting technique correctly before proceeding to the propulsive stage.

Arms

The arms should be allowed to *hang freely* by the sides. This has the effect of minimising tension in the upper body and allowing a relaxed position to be adopted. A tendency to hold the arms out obliquely may occur. This need not be detrimental (it does in fact increase the horizontal floating ability) providing they are not tensed. Where they are interfering with the comfortable position of the body—and this will usually be the case—they should be corrected.

Legs (Plates 16, 17 and 19)

The tendency of the legs is to sink in the majority of cases. The back-crawl leg kick and movement through the water helps to keep them horizontal. Faults likely to occur are given below and they can be interpreted in conjunction with the mechanical considerations:

(a) Kicking from the knee—usually resulting in limited or no propulsion even though the person is kicking. Depending also on the position of the feet, this may result in negative populsion, i.e. in the opposite direction to that intended. Verbal correction—by drawing the attention of the learner to the fault—will be found helpful. It is also useful to tell the learner to lift the water with his toes until the toes break the surface of the water and to keep the legs reasonably straight (Fig. 16).

(b) Kicking too deep—limited propulsion will be apparent, usually accompanied by an uncomfortable position in the water, tension and leg splashing. This fault often develops in conjunction with (a) and in the heavily built learner. Correction consists of emphasising a shallow relaxed leg kick and usually an increase in the speed of the kick.

(c) Ankles not extended—the mechanical analysis of the kick (page 73) indicates that most of the propulsion comes from the backward thrust on the water, due to the soles of the feet in the downward direction, and the instep of the foot in the upward direction. With the ankles flexed, a very limited area is available for propulsive force. When this fault occurs, the legs may appear to be kicking correctly, but with none or little forward movement. Attention to ankle position will usually correct the fault. N.B. Because of this unnatural strained position of the ankle it will often lead to signs of cramp in the back of the leg until the movement becomes more familiar.

(*d*) Too much flexion at knees—a small degree of flexion is desirable at the knee, to enable a relaxed leg kick. If this is overemphasised faults similar to (*a*) result, or with the kick from the thigh, the feet never come high enough to give their maximum propulsion. In general, it will be found that the leg kick develops with practice and passes through many of these fault stages. Other learners seem to be able to adopt the correct kicking action immediately.

Progression

In discussing the method, the learner was left at the stage of being able to adopt the correct back-lying position in a relaxed manner and to have started the leg kick. Progression from here will depend upon the individual learner. One of the difficulties which now presents itself is fear on the part of the teacher and not the learner. This is as it should be, and ensures that overconfidence does not lead to mishaps. Although the learner will be encouraged initially to practise his movements along the side of the bath where he can be reached by the teacher if necessary, it is desirable that he proceeds to cross the pool as soon as possible. This increases his own confidence and pleasure and prevents the distraction of colliding with the side of the pool. The teacher will naturally be worried about letting the learner (perhaps after only ten minutes) cross the pool alone. To overcome this difficulty, it has been found particularly helpful to take learners in pairs. When they have reached the stage of beginning to cross the pool, one will swim and the other will walk behind his head, very close but without actually touching him unless he is in difficulty (Plate 24). In the latter case, he will simply put his hands under the float and help the learner to stand up. In addition, when the learner is swimming across comfortably, his partner can warn him as he nears the other side of the pool whereupon he can stop his leg kick, allow his legs to sink and stand up. The teacher will be able to judge—although it is more likely that the learner will do it for him—when a partner is no longer necessary.

Although the list of faults outlined above may suggest that the learning of the back crawl leg kick and efficient propulsion of the beginner may take a long time, this is not in fact the case. It has been found for example that almost 100% of non-swimmers attending instruction at Leeds University during a one-year trial period could master an efficient propulsion on their back with floats on in one swimming session. Many had discarded their floats in the first session, and the majority by the end of the third session (these were students between the ages of 18 and 40 years).

Once the beginner has mastered the technique on the back with float inflated he is encouraged gradually to deflate the float as he gains confidence in his own ability. It is noticeable, and bears out the contention of lack of confidence previously expounded, that even when the float is fully deflated and contributing nothing to flotation, its very presence is sufficient to give confidence to the beginner! The transition from the float to without the float is always a critical one, but with encouragement and attention to the technique of starting off, this can be accomplished without a great deal of difficulty. It is sometimes the case that a person who has discarded the float on one session may have regressed in confidence by the next session. In such cases, floats should be available for them to wear if they wish to do so. This stage is usually quickly overcome.

Stroke Production

When the learner can swim, i.e. he is completely confident on his back, a choice is available to him. He can either leave instruction and rely on his own efforts to make progress on the front—which he will then have confidence to do fairly easily—or he can stay on to instruction in stroke techniques. The latter procedure will be developed in a later chapter. Once confident on his back, the swimmer is unlikely to experience any difficulty in making the transition to swimming on the front. Furthermore, it has been found that the swimmer can quickly acquire the technique of front crawl leg kick in a similar way and, moreover, that the kick acquired is both powerful and efficient (this will readily be observable in those swimmers who have been taught by the method suggested and continue with stroke production). There would appear to be positive transfer effects from swimming back crawl leg kick to swimming front crawl leg kick.

It might be asked at this stage, how long should the swimmer be kept on his back? This depends to a large extent on the swimmer himself and he should make the decision to move on to the front although very often help and encouragement in making such a decision will prove valuable. What must be borne in mind is that, before the swimmer transfers to the front, he should be *completely* confident on the back. In addition, he should 'know' what is meant by an extended ankle, a relaxed knee and ankle joint, kicking from the hips and a shallow fast kick with the feet just breaking the surface. Only when this level is reached will a smooth transfer be possible to the front crawl stroke.

16. *Fault 1.* Kicking too deep—legs should not come out of the water

17. *Fault 2.* Kicking with 'hooked' feet, i.e. ankles not extended—propulsion minimal or absent

18. *Fault 3.* Head lifted off the water giving an incorrect body-position with an increasing tendency for the legs to sink

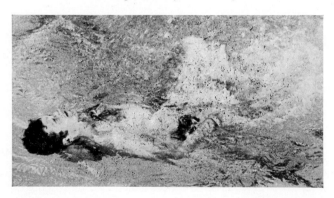

19. *Fault 4.* Kicking with bent knees

20. *Fault 5.* 'Sitting' in the water, brought about by failure to extend the hips

CHAPTER 4

Skill Learning

Although the teaching method discussed in the previous chapter has been concerned with acquiring skill, such skill has been acquired against a background of fear. For this reason, the method adopted has been used with the primary aim of counter-conditioning such fear while the technicalities of the skill itself have been accorded second place. This is one of the reasons why the propulsive skill on the back has been made as simple as possible. Arm movements have been excluded and the breathing problem largely eliminated. It was therefore considered less important to discuss principles of skill acquisition prior to the present stage of procedure. Now, having overcome the fear of the water and having acquired the ability to swim—in the sense of propulsion through the water with ease and confidence—it becomes necessary for those swimmers who wish to progress to acquire complex skills in the form of particular swimming strokes. The complexity of such skills is evidenced by the need to co-ordinate the sub-skills of kicking, breathing and the use of the arms. Moreover, such skills are learned against a background of already existing skills which may help, hinder, or have little effect on the current learning.

Although the principles of skill acquisition which are thought to be useful in the present context have not been elaborated in previous chapters, neither have they been completely ignored. Thus, under the heading of 'Putting the Swimmer in the Picture' in the preceding chapter, the *procedure* to be followed in the skill was discussed; *individual differences* within such a procedure were catered for by the comparative freedom given to the learner in getting into the required positions and initiating the leg kick.   *Knowledge of results* was emphasised as being essential to progress and the *mechanics* of the movement required were elaborated in an elementary way.   Such considerations now need to be discussed in more detail and their relevance recognised by the teacher.   In addition, it must be appreciated that swimming skills are relatively *'closed' skills* in Knapp's[1] terms.   A hint that *transfer of training* is involved in the changeover from back crawl to front crawl leg kick has already been implied.   The fact that so far only the leg kick has been taught and that this is a subskill of the complete stroke to which must be added and integrated sub-skills involving arm movements and breathing implies a consideration of *part-whole* learning.

Before therefore proceeding to stroke production, these topics will be given more detailed consideration in order that the relevant principles may be incorporated by the teacher into any stroke production methods adopted.

Procedure

Strictly speaking, procedural skills are those which involve a routine sequence of events such that once the sequence has been learned, the skill has in fact been acquired.   Examples of such skills are learning to programme an automatic washing machine for different fabrics or 'troubleshooting' in radio repairs where the operator knows little about washing machines or radio, but is able to carry out routine procedures in a sequential way. In such skills, the difficulty is not the actual manipulation itself, but in following the correct sequence of events. There is however another sense in which the description

[1] Knapp, B. *Skill in Sport*.   London: Routledge & Kegan Paul, 1964.

might apply to the type of skills presently being considered. Such skills—like any other skilled behaviour—involve a 'plan', an outline procedure of what follows what in the performance of the skill. This is how one swimming stroke can be differentiated from another and how errors in stroke production can be identified.

To know the procedure involved in a skill is an aid to learning, by-passing much of what is involved when a person has to experiment freely in a situation to discover such procedures completely for himself. (This is not to deny that once the procedure is established, free experimentation might not be a useful technique.) The ability to give procedural instructions verbally is one advantage that man possesses over the animal world. As a result, he can use such methods to cut short learning time.

The principle being discussed here was adopted in the previous chapter under the heading of 'Putting the Swimmer in the Picture'. An outline (plan) of the procedure to be adopted in getting on to the back and in propulsion through the water was given to the swimmer. By such means, it was hoped not only to allay some of the swimmer's fears, but to save time on instruction when he was in the water. Under such circumstances it is usually only necessary to draw the attention of the learner at the appropriate time to the instruction previously given. In doing so, it must be appreciated that the learner must not have been given too much to remember at once and there must not have been a long delay between the giving of the instruction and performing of the skill because of limitations in the short-term memory of the learner.

The reader will probably already have appreciated that giving procedural instructions is in many ways similar to the giving of a demonstration and emphasising the relevant importance of particular aspects of the skill. It would be wrong to suppose that in the latter circumstances, the learner *imitates* at some later stage the skill demonstrated to him. At least that is to say if by imitate is meant to copy exactly. What seems more likely is that the learner comes to appreciate the procedure involved in the skill and uses this as a basis for producing something *resembling* (but in no sense identical to) the skill demonstrated to him.

So far then, both verbal and visual methods have been suggested for giving such procedural outlines. They are not however the only methods. *Guidance* techniques have been shown to be useful in learning many skills and these were raised (page 37) in relation to the use of artificial aids. Such techniques usually involve either putting the learner physically through the movement which is required, or erecting such restrictions to movement that only the required movement can be carried out. In the past, there have been attempts to devise swimming machines for such purposes but these have in the main been costly and elaborate to little purpose. The machine in Figs. 18 and 19 for example was patented in America in 1896. To say the least, it looks formidable and one wonders what effect this would have on persistent non-swimmers! There is no indication that it was actually used. Teachers should not forego guidance procedures entirely. A little imagination might suggest simple guidance techniques which might be useful with particular individuals. It is not unusual for teachers actively to put their learner's arms or legs through a particular range of movement. This may be a useful adjunct to other procedures being adopted, but it should be remembered in so doing, that the pressure or restriction on the limb may alter the 'feel' of the movement to the learner and set him an 'image' to work on which is incorrect. In consequence he may well learn to discriminate but around an incorrect model. This point may be better appreciated in the context of 'body image' discussed later in the chapter.

The topic discussed in this section overlaps to some

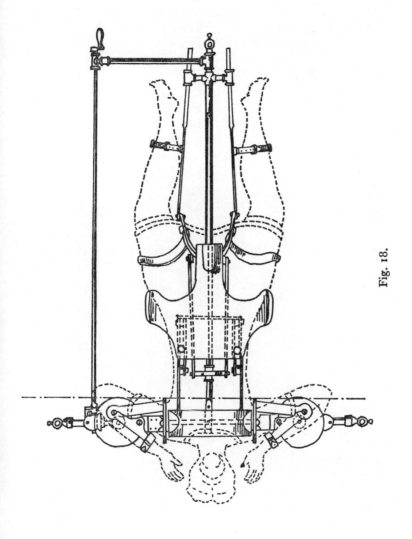

Fig. 18.

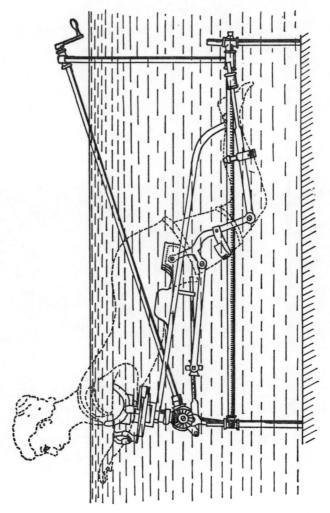

Fig. 19.

extent with the topic of the *mechanics* of the movement required. Although it is not appropriate to discuss the mechanics of a stroke with all swimmers, there are times when simple mechanical descriptions can give the learner a better knowledge of the procedure and a better 'image' of what he is trying to achieve. This was suggested in chapter 3 when the learner was told that he would be unlikely to be able to float horizontally—for mechanical reasons which were made explicit to him. Again, in discussing the back crawl leg kick, the propulsive power obtained with an extended ankle was dealt with.

Individual Differences

The study of individual differences is generally subsumed under the global heading of personality theory. It has already been found necessary to discuss certain personality theories in relation to *fear conditioning*. In a more fundamental way, it must also be understood that no one coming to the swimming situation starts entirely from scratch. Each individual possesses certain abilities, skills, biases which may help or hinder his progress. The teacher has to build on what has gone before. Thus, he must expect each learner to be different. In particular, in terms of physical ability it is expected that they will differ in initial standards, in their rate of learning and in their final level of attainment. In more mentalistic terms, they will differ in attitude, expectation, level of aspiration, trust, etc. It is only by appreciating such differences that the teacher can effectively carry out the task of teaching. This does not necessarily mean an entirely different method for each individual, but within any method(s) it does require sufficient flexibility to cope with such idiosyncrasies. The teacher needs to be tolerant and adaptive to varying circumstances.

In Chapter 2, some time was spent in elaborating Eysenck's theory of personality in relation to fear conditioning. This theory was thought to provide the most satisfactory explanation of the development of fear responses. There are of course many different theories of personality development. Psychologists such as Witkin[1] study personality through differences in the perceptual characteristics of individuals. It is not possible within the limits of this book to discuss their work in any great detail. These workers do however raise the interesting topic of what they term 'sophistication of body concept'. This is defined as:

'. . . the systematic impression the individual has of his body, cognitive and affective, conscious and unconscious formed in the process of growing up.'

Individuals differ in the degree of sophistication achieved, in their degree of differentiation of function of body parts and in the integrated working of the body as a whole. It may be more meaningful to the reader to think in terms of differences in 'body image'. While it would seem that movement experience contributes to the development of the body image (at an early age it is the fundamental determinant) it seems likely also that the possession of a sophisticated body-concept would be an aid to skill learning, but this has yet to be demonstrated.

It must of course be realised that experience in the 'foreign' medium of water will extend the body image because of the novel nature of the new experience and the consequent change in the signals fed back to the central nervous system by the body. The body *feels* different in the water. Movement experiences in the water differ from those on land because of the resistance of the water and changes in the gravitational effect. It is easy to over- or underestimate the extent, force or speed of the limb movement or the position of the limbs in water. The image of the body *is* different. This is one of the reasons

[1] Witkin, H. *et al. Psychological differentiation.* New York: Wiley, 1962.

why land drill is relatively ineffective. The experience of going through a stroke on land is not the same as in the water and it would not be surprising to find that little transfer of training occurred.

With additional experience the learner comes to 'know' his position in the water. He feels at home—orientated. It should also be noted that, initially, he needs to relate the novel sensations fed back from his body in the water to known frames of reference—other people in the pool, the sides and bottom of the pool, the roof etc. Later these cues will become redundant. The teacher can do much to speed up this process but only if he is aware of the fact that the learner is probably not experiencing the same sensations in the water as the experienced teacher would himself. Such considerations lead on naturally to the consideration of knowledge of results.

Knowledge of Results

It is not really possible in the performance of any skill to talk about *not* having any knowledge of results. Intrinsic knowledge of results is always present in some form or another. Take, for example, moving the arm with the eyes closed. It is not necessary for anyone to tell a person that his arm has moved. In addition he will have a pretty good idea of how far it has moved and in what direction. It might be argued that this is because he has moved it himself and therefore knew the direction and effort applied. But knowledge of results (feedback) is also available if someone else moves the arm for him. Usually, the eyes will be open so that in addition to 'feedback' via the receptors in the joints and tendons, visual information is available about the relative success of the skill carried out. In some skills, auditory or tactile information might also be important to the skill. Thus, feedback which is intrinsic to the skill is information which occurs as direct results of carrying out the skill itself and which can be utilised either in guiding ongoing behaviour or in correcting subsequent attempts at the skill.

In addition to feedback in this form, extra information can be given (extrinsic information) by, for example, a teacher. This information can be utilised in addition to any intrinsic feedback. Ultimately it will be necessary for the skill to be carried out without extrinsic knowledge of results so that the performer comes to rely on feedback which is intrinsic to the task or in the case of a proficient performer, the skill becomes so well developed (programmed) that the feedback information—at least at a conscious level—becomes unnecessary for carrying out the skill.

It has already been pointed out that during early experience in a water medium it is necessary for the person to reorientate himself—to get used to the new feelings and sensations which arise in the body because of the novelty of the experience. The intrinsic feedback resulting from the movement of a limb will differ from that present when the limb is moved out of water. The teacher can only be of help in this respect if he can communicate with the learner. In the method previously described, one of the advantages of being on the back was that the teacher and the external surroundings can be readily observed and knowledge of results becomes more meaningful. It is easier for the swimmer to learn to orientate himself and to 'know' what he is doing. Such information received at the time is not only good from an information point of view, but it is likely to result in greater positive motivation.

The teacher must not make the learner too dependent on his guidance in case he becomes too reliant on external sources of information and not on the feedback from his newly developing 'body image'.

Skills which rely on information from outside the body for their successful completion have been termed by

Knapp[1] *'open' skills*, while those which rely more on information from within the body are termed *'closed' skills*. It will be seen that, in the present context, swimming skills may start off as being relatively 'open' but as proficiency develops they become virtually 'closed' skills.

This comment raises an interesting point. It is tempting in teaching people any skill to observe what the expert in that skill does and to try to teach a similar performance to the beginner. This is often not successful for the simple reason that at the two levels of performance the skills are not the same. The crawl stroke attempted by the beginner is not just a scaled-down version of the stroke carried out by the expert. It is one of the anomalies of the situation that a beginner may be being taught a skill which he may not need to use when he is more proficient but it is a necessary stage through which he must pass on the way to approaching the final required performance!

Transfer of Training

By this term is meant the effect of learning one task on the effective performance of a subsequent task.

In most educational contexts, it is difficult to decide just what transfers and what does not. In the present context the situation is a little easier because interest lies in transfer of training in a relatively specific situation —from, for example, back crawl leg kick to front crawl leg kick and from back-floating to front-floating. While no objective evidence is available, it is maintained here that there is a marked positive transfer effect particularly if, while on the back *in the water*, the swimmer is made aware (by drawing his attention) of what an extended ankle, a relaxed knee, kicking from the hip, shallow kicking and horizontal position in the water mean.

[1] Knapp, B. *Skill in Sport.* London: Routledge & Kegan Paul, 1964.

Furthermore, it would seem pointless to look for structured experimental evidence for something which the teacher can prove for himself in a relatively short space of time providing the method has been followed.

It *might* be possible to discuss theoretically concepts like 'identical elements' within the two situations—if an element could be defined! Or draw attention to 'common principles' operating. A more useful comment here would seem to be in terms of what has been designated 'transposability of insight' implying that insight into characteristics of the performance of one task can transfer to another task where similar but not identical movements or principles are in operation. Thus, drawing the swimmer's attention to the factors discussed above while he is *in the water* gives insight at a proprioceptive[1] level which may transfer from the 'on the back situation' to that on the front. This will not make an immediate transfer possible but will shorten the time required to acquire the new skill.

Part-Whole Learning

Refers to the units into which a complex skill is divided for practice purposes. While with some skills it may be difficult to decide what comprises a unit, with complex swimming strokes the task would seem to be easier. Such skills seem to break down into units of leg kick, arm stroke and breathing. If these are practised in isolation, there still remains the difficult task of integrating such sub-skills into a composite whole. It may of course be possible to practise one of the sub-skills until it is proficient and then practise the next sub-skill in conjunction with that already acquired and so on. Workers in this field of learning tend to differ considerably as to whether part or whole learning is the better procedure and circumstances which particu-

---

[1] Refers to feedback from organs of balance as well as from the kinaesthetic sense organs in muscles, tendons and joints.

larly favour one or the other. If anything, experimental work has come down in favour of the 'whole' method but little work has been carried out on gross body skills. Again, such considerations as speed of learning, quality of performance and motivation of the learner have to be borne in mind in making any such decision. It is suggested that with the swimmers in question it is a better procedure—if one is interested in quality of stroke production—to proceed by the part method in which successive units are tagged on to those already learned. Thus, in learning the front crawl stroke, the leg kick will be acquired first. To this will be added the arm stroke and finally the breathing. When learning the back crawl procedure in the early stages, it will be remembered that both leg kick and breathing were practised together. The final stage consists in bringing in the arm action.

With the procedures discussed in the previous sections in mind, the teacher is ready to take the swimmer on to the development of a swimming stroke.

CHAPTER 5

Stroke Production

It might be argued that once beginners have learned to
swim on the back in the manner previously described,
they should be free to decide on which stroke they wish to
learn. This is a point with which the writer would not
disagree. Nevertheless, it is suggested that the most
logical and easiest progression is either on to the *full* back
crawl stroke or directly on to the front crawl stroke. For
this reason, this final chapter is concerned with progression in this manner for swimmers already taught by the
methods described in a previous chapter. The teacher
who wishes to proceed directly to breast-stroke or other
stroke should consult any standard swimming text but
with the suggestion that it might still be politic to get their
swimmers to practise the breast-stroke kicking action on
the back where knowledge of results can easily be given
as the stroke is progressing.

It must be reiterated here that it is advisable (depending upon time available, motivation of the swimmer etc.)
to delay further progress until the swimmer is completely
confident on the back. That is to say, when he has a
really efficient leg kick, can start and stop at will and is not
averse to an occasional splash of water over his face.
When this stage is reached the swimmer should be asked
how he would like to proceed (with some suggestion by
the teacher as to the alternatives, their advantages and the
length of time likely to be involved in developing a good

stroke). Many swimmers will be already satisfied with the stage reached and may want to opt out. If there is doubt about whether to go on to back crawl or front crawl first, it is useful to introduce the swimmer to the arm stroke for the back crawl and to see how he fares. Many swimmers are not happy in this situation even when competent on their back and will want to proceed to the front crawl stroke.

Back Crawl Stroke

The swimmer already has existing swimming habits in the form of an efficient leg kick, good body position and the ability to breathe freely. On to these habits has to be fitted an efficient arm stroke. There is, however, an anomaly here which will also occur in connection with the front crawl. The leg kick will be very powerful and capable of propelling the swimmer quickly across the pool. When he has learned to swim back or front crawl efficiently, the legs will only play a minimal role in propulsion, their principal function being that of maintaining the body in a relatively horizontal position thus minimising the braking effect of the legs when kept at an angle to the horizontal.

The procedure to be developed in adopting this stroke is as follows:

1. Put the swimmer in the picture by telling him the simple mechanics of the arm action (page 77), the need to keep the legs kicking in a relaxed and coordinated fashion and to breathe freely.

2. The swimmer should begin by swimming part way across the pool in the manner to which he has been accustomed and when he feels that he is progressing efficiently, he should attempt to bring in the arm action. There is little need to bother the swimmer with comments about coordination at this stage except in as far as it will have been described in the mechanics of the

stroke. Continued practice will generally result in such coordination being quickly achieved.

3. Many swimmers encounter difficulty in the form of swamping themselves with water. This can be minimised by encouragement to take the arms out of the water in a relaxed manner. In addition, they may at this stage be encouraged to raise their head a little so that their line of vision is towards their feet (providing that this does not cause a rotation which interferes with their leg kick).

4. A tendency to roll is often the outcome of reaching too far back with the arms. The correction is obvious. Swimmers sometimes need guidance as to the position of their arms as once again the changed 'body image' gives misleading impressions. It is useful to get the swimmer to brush his ear lightly with his arm. While useful from an information point of view it should not be maintained for more than guidance trials as it can lead to overreaching and a compromise solution may be necessary. The swimmer can of course see the teacher in this position and it is possible for him to give augmented knowledge of results either verbally or by gesticulation.

5. If there is a marked deterioration in the leg kick, it may be necessary to revert to an earlier stage for a period and reintroduce the arms at some later stage. It is pointless to proceed if the legs are sinking and the swimmer will do better to stop and start again. In some instances a reintroduction of the float can be of advantage.

6. The swimmer may revert to a previous fault of sitting in the water with a consequent breakdown in the whole stroke. This can be overcome by emphasis on relaxation (particularly of the abdominal muscles) and conscious attention to maintaining the horizontal position.

21. *Lying on the water, 1.* The 'swimmer' attempts the first stage of transferring on to the front

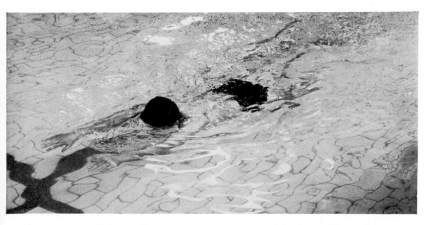

22. *Lying on the water, 2.* An improved body position

23. Pushing off from the side

24. Position to be adopted when walking at the head of a partner attempting to cross the pool on his back. Eyes always looking towards the swimmer, hands held ready but clear unless any difficulty is experienced

Front Crawl Stroke

It will be remembered that the swimmer will be progressing from either the stroke on which he originally learned or from the full back crawl stroke. In either case the procedure to be adopted is similar except that some modification may be in order for the swimmer who is already competent on the *full* back crawl stroke. Such modifications should be obvious to the teacher.

Swimmers are told that they will be progressing through a series of stages similar to those which they used in first learning to swim. The initial stages (given below) are described to them and the similarity between the front and back crawl leg kick (position, shallow kick from the hips, extended ankle, feet just breaking the surface, legs passing one another) emphasised. They will be set a target to achieve before the arms can be introduced. It is suggested that this be about ten yards to be covered on the front with the head in the water and without a breath.

Stages

1. In a similar way to that which was attempted on the back, the swimmer is to adopt a horizontal position on the front.[1] The swimmer puts his shoulders under the water, stretches his arms forward, puts his head gently in the water and leans forward until his feet come off the bottom. It does not matter how close the initial attempts resemble what is eventually required providing the basic procedure (plan) is followed. (Plate 21) The swimmer will quickly proceed to pushing forward and lying on the water. He should be encouraged to do so and to wait for his legs to sink before standing up. From the point of view of confidence, the swimmer should do this initial practice close to the edge of the pool but should be discouraged from holding on to the side.

[1] The 'float' is not now necessary.

F

Because the swimmer has obtained competence and sophistication in swimming on the back and has *himself chosen* to proceed to front crawl stroke, little difficulty will be found in performing this stage. An odd swimmer may have real difficulty—particularly if he has come too quickly off the back. If the method has been used with people who are not persistent non-swimmers, many of the stages described in the initial method and subsequently will be passed through very quickly.

2. When the swimmer can confidently adopt the front lying position with his arms on the surface, his head in the water and allow his legs to sink to the bottom (unless he is a floater in which case, a conscious effort will have to be made to stand up) he should progress by pushing himself off from the side of the pool in an effort to get progressively further each time. (Plate 23)

3. If confidence is established, the body position efficient and five or six yards covered each time, the swimmer should be encouraged to push off from the side *and once horizontal* to attempt the leg kick. He should also be encouraged to look at the bottom of the pool in an attempt to reach further and further across the pool. As might be expected, some swimmers have difficulty in getting the hang of the leg kick while others can make the transfer immediately. The swimmer should, however, be allowed to experiment for a reasonable period before correction is attempted. This should take the form previously described. It should be noted here, that knowledge of results can not now be given until the swimmer has finished his attempt. Thus it can only be useful for guiding subsequent attempts.

4. The swimmer should progress with this practice until the leg kick is proficient, relaxed, virtually automatic and can propel him at least ten yards without

able and willing to put into the cultivation of a good stroke. It is not intended to deal with all the faults which are likely to arise and their correction as it is not the primary intention of this book to produce really competent stroke swimmers. In the main, the ideas which have been developed throughout the book will be sufficient for a discerning teacher to base an efficient teaching programme and to make a difficult teaching situation both more profitable and more pleasurable.

Mechanics of the Front and Back Crawl Strokes

1. LEG KICK (Figs. 20, 21)

With slight variations, the principles involved in both the back and front crawl strokes are the same. The propulsive power developed by the leg kick will be more important in the early stages of learning the strokes, and with swimmers lacking a powerful arm action. With the more proficient swimmer, the emphasis on the propulsive power of the leg kick will be decreased. But from the point of view of efficiency of action, it is likely that the leg position will remain similar in both cases to avoid the 'braking' action which would result from a failure to extend the ankle (Fig. 22) or from kicking too deep.

As far as swimming strokes are concerned, the important mechanical law is Newton's third law of motion:

'To every action there is an equal and opposite reaction.'

In order for the body to be propelled forward it is necessary for a force to be exerted by the body in pushing the water backwards. This may be brought about by the action of the arms or the legs in isolation or by a combination of the two. In addition, the momentum attained in a forward direction will equal the momentum of the water pushed backwards. The question which thus arises is

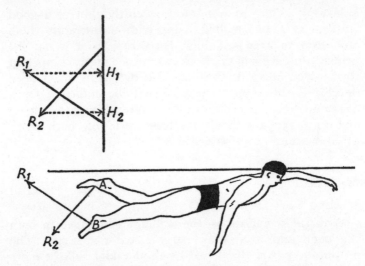

Fig. 20. Forces exerted in the front crawl leg action.

the most efficient method of producing a backward thrust on the water.

Cureton[1] as long ago as 1930 carried out an extensive analysis of the front crawl leg kick.   While in theory, it is possible for propulsion to come from the effort applied to the water by the thigh, lower leg or foot, in practise it is clear that the *major* propulsive force comes from the foot itself acting at the extremity of a long lever arm.   For both front and back crawl leg kicks, with the legs working in a mechanically efficient position, propulsion occurs from both the down and the up kick.   The amount of propulsion in both cases is dependent upon the angle which the foot makes with the surface of the water. Again, Cureton was able to demonstrate that the maximum propulsive force comes from the up beat (kick) in

[1] Cureton, T. K. Mechanics and kinesiology of swimming. *Res. Quart.* 1, 40, 1930.

the front crawl. While it does not appear to have been demonstrated for the back crawl leg kick, observation and experience would seem to suggest that with the shallow kick being advocated it is the down kick which contributes the greatest propulsive force (Fig. 21). Part of the effectiveness of the foot action is due to the relatively large surface area of the foot which is acting on the water. Maximum force is obtained by presenting as large a surface area as possible in the opposite direction to that of the desired movement coupled with a fast and powerful

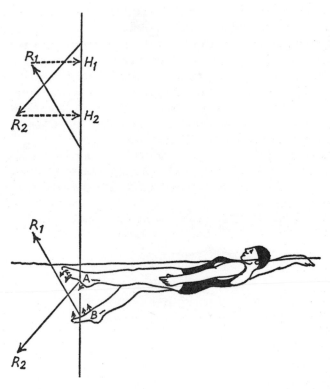

Fig. 21. Forces exerted in the back crawl leg action.

action. The effect of a change in the surface area is most noticeable when 'flippers' are added to the feet and the front or back crawl leg kick carried out.

Figs. 20 and 21 illustrate the direction of the forces acting on the water due to the up and down beat of the feet and their resultants R_1 and R_2 (big arrows) in the direction indicated. In the force diagram, the vector H_1 represents the resultant force in propelling the body *forwards* due to the up beat and H_2 the resultant force due to the down beat. As foot A begins to move downwards, the angle made by force R_2 with the vertical decreases. Now the effective backward horizontal thrust is proportional to the sine of this angle. Thus, as the foot moves down the angle decreases and hence so does the horizontal thrust. The down beat contributes its maximum effect early in the beginning of its action. In a similar way, the decreasing effect of the up beat as the foot moves upwards can be accounted for. It is of course possible to adjust the angle of the foot by either flexing or extending the ankle as the kick proceeds or by bending the knee more. In the latter case, the efficiency of the kick will be affected (by shortening of the lever arm) and the braking effect increased.

When the feet are 'hooked' (Fig. 22) they do not con-

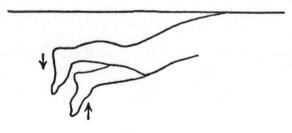

Fig. 22.

tribute anything to forward movement of the body and little to keeping the legs up, since the horizontal force component is zero and the surface area presented to the water relatively small.

It will be noted from this brief discussion that the kick as a whole is a compromise between an increasing effectiveness in terms of angle presented to the water obtained by bending the knee and extending the kick over a longer distance and the prevention of a braking effect due to the legs being too low in the water and kicking too slowly. This would appear to involve a relaxed but only slightly bent knee, an extended but flexible ankle and a shallow and fast kick from the hips.

Armed with these minimal ideas about the mechanical efficiency of the leg kick, the coach will be in a better position to help in developing in his swimmer an effective propulsive kick.

2. *Arm Action* (Fig. 23)

As with the leg action, from the point of view of efficiency, it is desirable to have the lever at maximum length when exerting its pull in a direction which will result in forward propulsion. Unlike the leg kick, there is a recovery phase in the arm action when it will be desirable to shorten the lever arm so that any negative propulsive force will be reduced to a minimum. With both the front and back crawl arm action, a propulsive force in a forward direction is only produced during the middle portion of the action (Fig. 23). When the arms first enter the water and if they are kept straight the propulsive force is in an upward direction tending to lift the body out of the water and make its progress a series of ups and down. This can be overcome to some extent in the front crawl by letting the fingers enter the water first by bending the wrist. In the front crawl a compromise has to be reached between the lift which occurs when a straight arm entry is used and the shortening of the lever arm when the fingers enter the water first

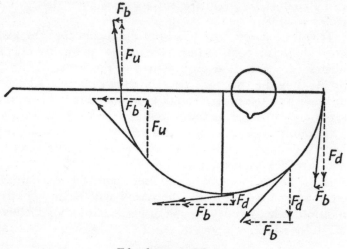

Fd = downward force
Fb = backward force
Fu = upward force

Fig. 23. Direction and magnitude of components of equal forces applied at various points on an arc (Broer 1966)

and the arm is consequently bent. With the racing swimmer, the maximum lever arm is probably the greatest consideration and he may put up with any lift due to entering the water with a relatively straight arm. With the learner, it may be better to compromise in favour of fingers entering the water first. The writer is not however convinced of this and feels that individual differences will be the determining factor here. With those people who are able to provide a powerful arm action it may be desirable to use the straight arm pull from the beginning. As the arms pull through past the vertical there is an increasing tendency to exert an upward force against the water resulting in the body being forced downwards and adding once again to the up and down movement. It will be an advantage for the learner to shorten the lever arm by bending the arm. This will also result in a decrease in the surface area presented to the water. Some of the effectiveness of the arm stroke can be wasted if the pull results in a sideways movement. This may occur when the arms do not enter the water approximately level with the shoulders in the front crawl or when a high reach overhead is carried out in the back crawl action. In addition allowing the arms to move across the body in the effective phase of the front crawl action will result in rotation of the body in the water which may upset the stroke and impede progress.

The back crawl arm action will result in a shallower pull than that of the front crawl because of the mechanical difficulties involved at the shoulder joint. There is thus less tendency to lift the body out of the water or cause it to sink and the effective propulsive force can be maintained over a greater distance by suitable flexion of the wrist as the arms move towards the sides.

Acknowledgements

My thanks are due to:

American Medical Association for permission to reproduce a figure from the Journal of Diseases in Children by D. E. Zook (Fig. 1).

American Association for Health, Physical Education and Recreation for permission to reproduce figures from articles in the Research Quarterly by H. T. A. Whiting (Figs. 7, 8, 9 & 10).

U.S. Department of Commerce for kindly supplying the material for Figs. 18 & 19 from a patent taken out by James Emerson.

M. Braham for the photography which resulted in the Plates (University of Leeds Dept. of Photography).

M. C. Winterton for acting as a subject for the photography.

W. B. Saunders Co., and Marion Broer for permission to reproduce a figure from 'Efficiency of Human Movement' (Fig. 23).

Irene Glaister of the Dept. of Physical Education, Leeds University for critical reading of the manuscript.

G. T. Adamson of the Dept. of Physical Education, Leeds University, for critical reading of the proofs.

References

(*Numbers in brackets indicate the pages in the text where the reference is introduced.*)

Behnke, A. R. *et al.* The specific gravity of healthy men. *J. Americ. Medical Assoc.*, 118, 1942 [4].

Bentler, P. M. An infant's phobia treated with reapproval inhibition therapy. *J. Child. Psych. & Psychiat.*, 3, 1962 [28].

Cureton, T. K. Mechanics and kinesiology of swimming. *Res. Quart.*, 1, 40, 1930 [74].

Davies, M. B. The specific gravity of the human body. Unpublished Master's thesis, Wellesley College, 1930 [4].

Eysenck, H. J. *The biological basis of personality.* London: Routledge & Kegan Paul, 1968 [27].

Highmore, G. *et al.* Initial investigation into the nature of flotation. *Physical Educ. J.*, 148, 1955 [4].

Highmore, G. *et al.* The problem of the male non-floater. *Physical Educ. J.*, 148, 1957 [4].

Knapp, B. *Skill in sport.* London: Routledge & Kegan Paul, 1964 [54].

Mowrer, O. H. *Learning theory and the symbolic process.* New York: Wiley, 1960 [23].

Pavlov, I. P. *Conditioned reflexes.* London: O.U.P., 1927 [25].

Rozelle, R. & Hellebrandt, F. The floating ability of women. *Res. Quart.* 8, 1937 [5].

Sandon, F. A preliminary enquiry into the density of the living human body. *Biometrika*, 16, 1924 [3].

Spivak, C. D. The specific gravity of the human body. *Archives of Intern. Medic.*, 15, 1915 [3].

Stembridge, D. E. & Whiting, H. T. A. Personality and the persistent non-swimmer. *Res. Quart.*, 36, 3, 1965 [31].

Watson, J. B. & Rayner, R. Conditioned emotional reactions. *J. Exp. Psych.*, 3, 1920 [25].

Whiting, H. T. A. Variations in floating ability with age in the male. *Res. Quart.*, 34, 1963 [7].

Whiting, H. T. A. Variations in floating ability with age in the female. *Res. Quart.*, 36, 1965. [7].

Witkin, H. *et al. Psychological differentiation.* New York: Wiley, 1962 [60].

Zangwill, O. L. *An introduction to psychology.* London: Methuen, 1950 [23].

Zook, D. E. The physical growth of boys. *Am. J. Diseases of Child.* 43, 1932 [5].

Index